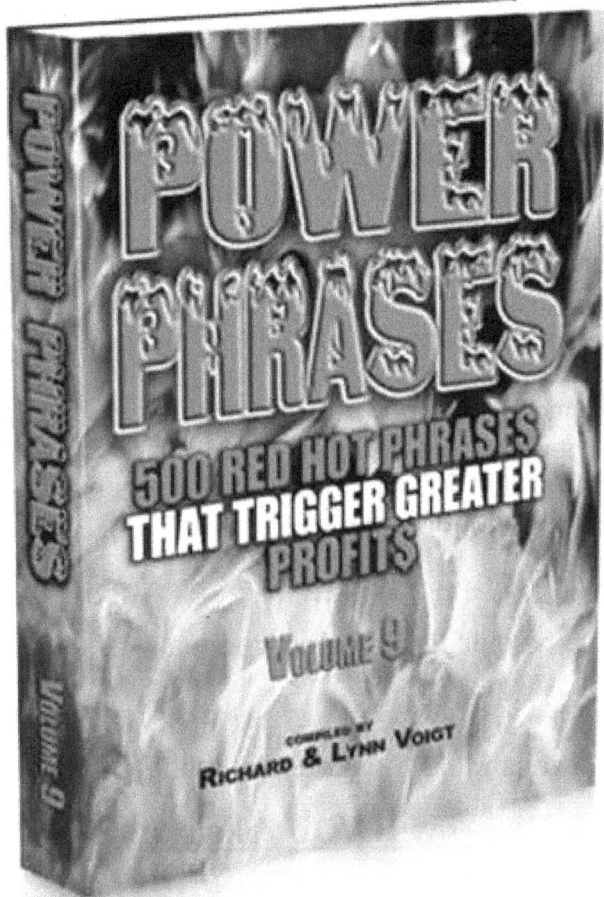

POWER PHRASES – Vol. 9
500 Power Phrases That Trigger Greater Profits

ISBN-13: 978-1-940961-08-8
ISBN-10: 1940961084

First Printing, 2013

Printed in the United States of America

To Access More Powerful Marketing Tools Visit:

www.RIVObooks.com

www.RIVOinc.com

www.WisconsinGarden.com

POWER PHRASES

Volume 9

500 POWER PHRASES THAT TRIGGER GREATER PROFITS

-·|·-•·*”””*·•·-·|·-•**•-·|·-•·*”””*·•-·|·-

Compiled by

Richard & Lynn Voigt
I.M. Education Specialists

Introduction:

Powerful Phrases, Headlines, Sub Headlines, Slogans, Bullet Points and Interview Sound Bites are perhaps the most powerful marketing tools mankind has ever created. They are the lifeblood behind every business venture are the ultimate secret weapon of Millionaire Marketers.

No matter whether you are introducing or promoting a brand new product, teaching a "How To" skill, building a website, or simply sending an email, using the perfect power phrase is crucial to capturing and holding eyeballs and producing greater marketing profits.

In today's world every word you use has measurable impact. Each word can produce emotional psychological buttons that trigger psychological reactions. Successful advertisers understand that using an effective power phrase is a true art form that turns "wants" into instant gratification "needs." Once artfully triggered, any niche market can instantly create more protifable conversions.

Now it's your turn to personalize this incredible collection of 500 Power Phrases in ways that instantly advance your own effective marketing skills as you create new and power phrases, slogans, presentations, bullet points, or interview sound bites that take you to the next level.

Whether starting or running a small business, writing an ad, coming up with a memorable slogan, making a major corporate presentation, bullet points, creating a video, writing a book, searching for the perfect slogan, teaching a lesson or book report, your creative use of these Power Phrases can capture more eyeballs and produce some amazing rewards quickly turning you into a Marketing Genius. Now, it's your turn to make the magic happen!

POWER PHRASES

Volume 9 – 4001 - 4500

500 Power Phrases That Trigger Greater Profits

Begin Selecting & Customizing Your Perfect Marketing Phrase

4001	I Created This Out Of Frustration
4002	Define Your Target Market
4003	Why Can't You Just Tell Me Everything All At Once
4004	Rely On Your Trusted Partners
4005	Form Your Own Corporation Without An Attorney
4006	Don't Allow Your Creative Muscles To Atrophy
4007	Receive 100 Ideas Every 7 Days
4008	Name You ME-ME
4009	It's Now Up And Running
4010	Get Higher Clicks And Better Conversions By Joining Today
4011	Here's Our Latest Video
4012	It's Just Too Easy Not To Get Successful Results
4013	The Key Ingredient
4014	That's Pure Bull Skin
4015	We All Do It For The Love Of It
4016	I'll Personally Answer Your Marketing Questions
4017	Laugh Giggle Or Groan
4018	You Think I Might Be An Axe Murderer
4019	Wish You Were Here
4020	Cash Back Reward Based Advertising
4021	Test Drive This One For Yourself

4022	Get Your Hands On My Update
4023	How Foreign Policy Effects You
4024	Fast Track To Earning Money Online
4025	Running An Information Marketing Business
4026	What Is It That You Absolutely Must Have Right Now
4027	Run Down A Complete History
4028	More Than Just The Facts
4029	If We Could Only Have It Done For Us
4030	Without The Technology You'll Never Know
4031	You're The Person To Give It To Them
4032	Strengthen You Core Muscles
4033	Your Unconscious Mind
4034	What's Going On
4035	You're Going To Be Grateful I Taught You This
4036	I Know The Process You're Going Through
4037	Access To Consult Someone In Authority
4038	Position Yourself As An Instructor
4039	Promoting Affiliate Programs Is Only One Business Strategy
4040	My Secret Diary
4041	Stop Editing Your Spoken Thoughts
4042	Brand New Markets
4043	You Get What You Pay For
4044	Different Approach And Solution In One
4045	Young And Foolish
4046	Just Sitting In Front Of Your Computer
4047	Let The Stress Finally Vanish
4048	The Secret Of Making People Like You
4049	Fools Recklessly Believe
4050	What To Do With Your Hands
4051	Avoid The Crap Cluttering The Marketplace
4052	Dance The Night Away While Your Business Grows
4053	As I Share These Truths
4054	For The Past Several Years
4055	You'll Need These Tools To Succeed
4056	The World Judges You
4057	Natural Modern And Creative
4058	Learn How To Protect It
4059	Log Into Your New Account

7

4060	Selling Your Foreign Language Rights
4061	This Makes Me Sick
4062	Putting Your Website On Audio Autopilot
4063	Get Others To Endorse You
4064	Are You Missing Something
4065	Generate Profits Online
4066	What Skills Should You Have In Producing Teleseminars
4067	All Out War - Are You Ready
4068	The Most Rewarding Things I Do
4069	Narrowing vs. Generating Options
4070	I'm Not Too Embarrassed To Admit It
4071	Where To Go From Here
4072	Accidental vs. Intentional
4073	Up To The Minute Sales Data
4074	Proactive Team Work
4075	Invisible Buy Buttons
4076	Whether Or Not To take Action
4077	Got The Answers
4078	List Building Problems
4079	You Never Dreamt Of This Before
4080	Dance And Stretch
4081	It's A Great Time To Be A Writer
4082	Don't Just Stay Where You Are - Leap The Competition
4083	Mouth To Mouth Promotion
4084	Key Ways To Raising Money The Easy Way
4085	You're Now In The Very Best Company
4086	A Report You've Been Anticipating
4087	Seize The Power
4088	Get Affiliates To Fall In Love With You And All Of Your Offers
4089	Don't Roll Over This Week And Play Dead
4090	Free Emotional Tune-Ups
4091	Secrets That Drive Men Wild
4092	Chat With Our Team
4093	Return To The Resting Position
4094	From A Standing Start
4095	Avoid Mistakes - Aim Your Business In The Right Direction
4096	Home Based Business Is The Wave Of The Future
4097	Relabeling Your Nerves

4098	Secret Bonus Section
4099	Bidding Too Much Or Too Low
4100	Streamline And Portable
4101	Fun Is A Big Core Value
4102	Adding Twice The Value
4103	If You Can Read This You Can Follow This Plan
4104	Never Look Back
4105	Cash In On Digital Trash
4106	This Will Change The Face Of Internet Marketing
4107	The Mortal Headline Sin
4108	Advance Testing Systems That Pull Subscribers In
4109	Why This Is So Irresistible
4110	Enlighten Your Readers
4111	Can't Make This Insane Offer Available Forever
4112	Get In Early
4113	Proud To Be My Own Boss
4114	They Said It Was Easy
4115	Better Results Mean More Profits
4116	Google Has Changed
4117	Raining Cash From The Sky
4118	Here Is Exactly How To Succeed With Safelists
4119	Not Long After The Ink Dries
4120	Forget The Camera
4121	Make An Appointment
4122	Visual Presentation Converting The Best
4123	Traffic Exchanges Take Too Long
4124	Engage Them Into The Next Step
4125	Dancing For Joy
4126	No Email Address Required
4127	Why Pre-Foreclosures Are The Best Profit Opportunity
4128	Giving You The Best Price
4129	Examine Them Carefully
4130	Use The Right Psychological Triggers
4131	Extra Pay Every Weekend
4132	Never Come Up Short Again
4133	$2,750 Per Month Part-Time
4134	How To Build An Empire
4135	Who's Really Reading Your Manuscript

9

4136	Skip The Frustration
4137	You're Not Invited
4138	That's Not Where They're At
4139	How A Simple Formula Can Become A Laser Beam
4140	Maximize Your Genius
4141	Will Next Year Really Be Different For Your Business
4142	Frustrated Broke And Ready To Quit
4143	Natural Born Leader
4144	Internet Marketing Is In A Constant State Of Flux
4145	Secret Of Perceived Value
4146	How To Protect Your Identity Online
4147	Magnified Future Prosperity
4148	So Easy A Caveman Could Do It
4149	Download And Profit
4150	This Vicious Cycle Can Be Avoided
4151	Remain Completely Anonymous If You Wish
4152	Don't Lose Your Imagination
4153	Start Small And Build Traffic
4154	Interested In Oldies
4155	Here's What's Happening
4156	Give Me Freedom And Independence Every time
4157	Skyrocket Your Delivery Sales
4158	They Aren't Bad Yet
4159	Addicted To Productivity
4160	Making It More Than That
4161	Taking Full Responsibility For Managing My Time
4162	Work Smart Be Clever And Make Money
4163	If You're Broke Then You Need Us
4164	Permanently Dismantling
4165	Rambunctious Newbies
4166	Risk Is Minimal
4167	Wants + Needs Foster Solutions = Sales
4168	The Internet Has Changed Everything
4169	I Just Found This "No Crash" Hosting Solution
4170	Success In A Proven Mentor
4171	Can You Still Fit Into Your Skinny Marketing Jeans
4172	Time vs. Money
4173	An Eye Opening Journey Into The Abyss

4174	Create Life-Long Financial Independence
4175	Extract The Best Material
4176	You Read The Headlines And Nobody Believes It
4177	Offer These As A Bonus
4178	Built In Feed Back Loops
4179	Has History Taught Us This
4180	How Do You View Social Networking
4181	Weird Pricing Competition
4182	Why Has My Life Become So Dependent On Money
4183	Ridiculously Effective
4184	Time To Check Your Style Sheet
4185	Guaranteed Lowest Price
4186	If It's Important You'll Make The Time
4187	Nerves And Nervousness
4188	The Seven Deadly Sins Of Website Copy
4189	Are All Business People Dishonest
4190	Keep Your Hair Off Your Face
4191	Why's That A Difficult Decision
4192	Don't Leave Just Yet
4193	Cracking The Information Monopoly
4194	Get Your Thinking Around Their Wants
4195	Reinforce Your Credibility
4196	Enhance Your Abilities
4197	Competitors Bumping Your Sales
4198	Feel Great In Seconds Not Minutes
4199	It Looks Like It Was Made Just For Me
4200	A Completely Unique Approach To Cashing In
4201	Your Marketing Hope Diamond
4202	Great Places Products and Services
4203	Producing Content
4204	This Is Pure Gold
4205	No Money Down Can Work
4206	Why These Don't Reply On Luck
4207	Even In A Faltering Economy Creative Opportunities Exist
4208	Not A Technical Wizard What Could You Accomplish With One
4209	Your Direct Link To Success Is But A Click Away
4210	Do You Question Your Assumptions
4211	Weight Losing Guide

11

4212	One Little Bonus I Forgot To Mention
4213	Don't Miss Today's Deadline
4214	Here's How To Boost Business Profits
4215	Moving Monday Magic
4216	Watch The Magic Happen
4217	This Has Its Own Life
4218	Designed With Sales Triggers
4219	Limited Copies So Order Today
4220	A Dozen New Ways To Outlive Your Doctor
4221	Do Your Headlines Suck
4222	Pushy Prospectors
4223	I Don't Like To Work
4224	Affiliate Making Money Systems
4225	The Sweet Spot
4226	So What Is Real Wealth
4227	Can You Top This
4228	Avoiding Information Overload
4229	Why Others Totally Miss This
4230	Still Not Thrilled With Your Website
4231	Trigger Their Emotional Hot Buttons
4232	Real Strategies You Wished Someone Had Told You About
4233	Paid Instantly - WOW - Hundreds Of Dollars
4234	7 Tips To Expand Your Marketing Skills
4235	You've Got To Offer Something Unique
4236	How To Tell The World About It
4237	Problem Solvers Will Be In High Demand
4238	These Ads Must Work
4239	Should I Merge My Newsletter And Blog
4240	What Are All The Fears Your Customer Is Having
4241	I Need You To Start Making Money
4242	The Physical Brain Hates Failure
4243	Where Skepticism Is Unhealthy
4244	Angles To Eliminate Objections
4245	Breathe And Relax
4246	Lead With A Powerful Sentence
4247	Here Are The Juicy Details
4248	Create Ways To Survey Customer's Desires
4249	Works For What Ever You're Selling

4250	A Friend Is Always There When He Needs You
4251	Portal Technology That Rocks
4252	The Never Ending Challenge
4253	We've Taken All The Guesswork Out
4254	I Know This Is Going To Work
4255	Less Scary Than Originally Thought
4256	Accelerate Your Success - Upgrade Your Order
4257	Nature Of The Soul
4258	A Great Mini Series Of Critical Information
4259	How Did You Go Through The Process
4260	I'll Never Make This Rookie Mistake Again
4261	Disgusted Buttlegging
4262	Sales Have Never Come So Fast
4263	Calculated Purposeful And Effective
4264	Why You Need To Create Links
4265	Last 30 Days
4266	Time To Bounce Back Big Time
4267	Don't Let Them Burn You
4268	Put It On Your T-Shirt
4269	Targeted Opt-In Safe List Kicks Butt
4270	Learning New Ways To Slice And Dice It
4271	I Love Educating People About This
4272	Guard Dog Hungry And Available
4273	All You Need Is Something That Works
4274	Time To Topple Old Taboos
4275	Words Are What Men Live By
4276	There's Always Something To Write About
4277	How Marketing Could Get You Blacklisted
4278	Gain An Unfair Advantage Over Them
4279	Where To Find The Best Streaming Video Websites
4280	My Job Is To Educate You
4281	Give This Some Serious Thought
4282	You'll Need To Dig Deeper
4283	Get Onboard To Live The Life You Want
4284	My New Year Blowout
4285	Power Of Repeat Sales
4286	I Think On Purpose
4287	Strategies That Create The Highest Long Term Profits

13

4288	Center Yourself Before Starting
4289	Unprecedented Economic Freedom
4290	Ability And Fortitude
4291	Can Something So Powerful Be So Simple
4292	Earn Revenue From Your Default Ads
4293	Building Ours From Home
4294	Create Viral Cloaked Links
4295	Perfect For Non-Moving Bootays
4296	This Can Never Be Recovered
4297	Then What's The Point
4298	We Handle The Technical Side
4299	Put A Price Tag On And Tell Them
4300	See What You've Been Missing
4301	Satisfy This One Small Desire
4302	You Can't Be In Your Head Here
4303	Get This Free Internet Biz Guide Now
4304	Be Real And Believable
4305	Add Your Own Unique Spin
4306	Immediately Remember Each And Every Word
4307	It Wasn't An Overnight Success
4308	Split Testing System
4309	We All Want To Be Interesting Human Beings
4310	We Close The Cart
4311	If You Love Being In Complete Control
4312	Great Place For Key Point Anchors
4313	Generating Massive Wealth Is A Reality
4314	Listen To Honest Feedback
4315	Let's Have A Marketing Affair
4316	Download Your Free Copy Right Now
4317	Gain The Perspective To Be A Leader
4318	I Absolutely Love Math
4319	Need More Than Just A Little Extra Each Month
4320	Something That's Safe And Easy
4321	We Fixed It
4322	Why Mornings Are More Productive
4323	Why I Still Do What I Do
4324	Rake In Millions Of Dollars Every Year
4325	What 10 Years Online Has Taught Me

4326	Remember These 5 Copywriting Formulas
4327	Now You Can Create Multiple Accounts
4328	Your Double Edge Sword
4329	Identify And Personalize Your Strategies
4330	I'm A Huge Fan Of Virtual Real Estate
4331	Unspoken Tactic That Captures Thousands Of Quality Backlinks
4332	A Name You Can Trust Online And Offline
4333	Do You Really Know Your Customers
4334	High Priced Products That Create A Steady Flow Of Customers
4335	Marketing Sugar Rush
4336	List Building Basics
4337	You Can Have It All
4338	Without Spending A Dime
4339	A Profitable Revenue Sharing System
4340	Hard To Keep Success A Secret
4341	What Are Those Twinkling Lights
4342	Are You Part Of The Inner Circle Yet
4343	Buy One Get One Free
4344	Create Instant PDF
4345	Easy To Use
4346	Big Tip Makes Money
4347	Being Hounded From Every Direction
4348	No More Than 15 Minutes Of Their Attention
4349	Knock Down Dream Blocking Barriers
4350	Leader Wanted
4351	Grab Yours Before This Price Expires
4352	Don't Tuck Your Headlines In The Sand
4353	This Is Not The You Show
4354	Reunion Notification
4355	The Article Beyond Description
4356	Included As A Special Bonus
4357	An Easier Method Of Making Money
4358	Ever Been Accused Of Insanity
4359	Getting It Out There And Marketing It
4360	That's What You Wanted
4361	What Happens When You Ask The Right Questions
4362	Implementation Is More Important Than The Product
4363	Max It Out

15

4364	Your Final Notice
4365	Make A Fortune Off Of Ignorance
4366	Listen To A Free Sample
4367	I Want To Claim My Spot
4368	It Should Be An Irresistible Offer
4369	The Tradition Continues
4370	Don't Ignore The Power Behind SEO
4371	This Revolutionized The World
4372	Putting 1 And 2 Together
4373	Why Money Doesn't Equal Power
4374	Should Really Get You Excited
4375	Selling Isn't A Dirty Word
4376	How Good Is This Product You Tell Me
4377	Magical Recipe For Making Money Online
4378	Step Into The Moment
4379	Links Above Are Also The Sources.
4380	Final 2 Days
4381	Build Passive Advertising Sources
4382	Watch Your Business Grow
4383	Don't Spend Any More Money
4384	Marketing Kiss Of Death
4385	Every Problem Has Unlimited Solutions
4386	See What You Can Do For Them In Return
4387	Bypass Survival And Failure
4388	Can You Generate Traffic From This
4389	We're Only A Phone Call Away
4390	These Hold The Secrets
4391	Marketing Pleasure Or Pain
4392	Do You Realize Your True Potential Can Change Your Future
4393	Emotionally Powerful Stuff
4394	I Could Tell You All Kinds Of Wonderful True Stories
4395	Product Landing Pages
4396	A Pure Blast Of Creative Genius
4397	Stuff Dragging You Down
4398	Massive Commission Opportunity
4399	Does This Sound Like You
4400	Keyword Generating Sales Not Clicks
4401	Why This Idea Really Works

16

4402	Don't Settle For Minnow Traffic
4403	Reaching For Words
4404	Silly Holiday Specials
4405	What's The Truth
4406	Why Medium Earth Tone Colors Work Best
4407	It's Your Birthright
4408	Delay May Be Serious
4409	Makes Self-Publishing A Breeze
4410	Miraculous Keys Reveal Unlimited Creativity
4411	Identify Your Magic Zone
4412	Why Their Wallet Becomes Secondary
4413	Blowout Tornado Sale
4414	Representing People's Identities
4415	Garden Flower Blanket
4416	Ad Placements Not Just Anywhere
4417	Instant Turkey Business
4418	Check Out All These Videos
4419	Blown Away By The Whole Prospect
4420	Making Money With A Website
4421	Be A Winner Today
4422	Register While Seats Still Available
4423	Dynamic Copycatting
4424	Whose Fault Is It When Children Disobey
4425	Why People Aren't Having Success Fast Enough
4426	And Why Aren't You Making Money
4427	Yes It Costs Money To Learn
4428	Change Your Life This Year
4429	Wonder Products Still Not Making You Money
4430	Use That Data
4431	How The New Mobile Culture Can Do Business Anywhere
4432	Create Personal Mission Statements
4433	Build Your Own Lists
4434	Punch Your Golden Ticket
4435	The Pivotal Mistake
4436	Energy Flows Where Attention Goes
4437	New Ideas Pop Up Every Day
4438	The One And Only Magic Formula
4439	An Online System You Can Afford

4440	Use Price Increases To Create Scarcity
4441	Wasted Ads
4442	What Kind Are You Going To Make
4443	But Only Men With Imagination Can Take It
4444	We're Getting So Many Inquiries
4445	Advertise With Style Using Timeless Ads
4446	Don't Know What To Say
4447	They Literally Sell Themselves
4448	Self Organizational Learning
4449	This Huge Market Is Growing Fast
4450	5 Fast Ways To Explode Your Opt-In List
4451	Your Video Journal
4452	My Ultimate Money-Making Strategic System
4453	How To Always Turn A Profit
4454	Search Engine Ranking Factors
4455	Brag Some More
4456	Online Coaching Offers Big Educational Opportunities
4457	Is That Really True
4458	Mentally And Psychologically Engage Your List
4459	Business Gets Done In Person
4460	Start A Daily Video Journal
4461	Last Minute Shopping
4462	The Customer Advantage
4463	Wealthy Behavior
4464	Keys To Success
4465	More Money For The Same Work
4466	This Will Make You Feel Powerful
4467	Time Flies When You're Making Money
4468	Secrets For Income Acceleration
4469	Commence Typing
4470	Discover This Tasty Gem
4471	Strategically Add Testimonials
4472	You Can't Make Sales If You Don't Have Customers
4473	You Won't Want To Cancel This Membership Ever
4474	Starting Before You're Ready
4475	Generate Sites Faster Smarter & Cheaper
4476	Your Life Can Change Dramatically
4477	In The Zone

18

4478	I Make Money Online
4479	How Shall I Fill My Time Now
4480	That's Not An Effective Way To Market
4481	Moral Hazard Heading Your Way
4482	Still Keeps The Money Rolling In
4483	Have You Updated Yet
4484	Walk You Through The Main Overview
4485	Overcome Dismal Results
4486	Lethal Power Of The Hole Punch Method
4487	Did I Finally Get This Idea Through To You
4488	You'll Never Be Left On Your Own Ever Again
4489	Making New Connections
4490	Huge Money Maker
4491	Break It Down Into Easy
4492	Perhaps You Would Love To Own This
4493	Getting Your Business Off The Ground
4494	Here's The Full Range Of Benefits
4495	Be Committed With Your Story
4496	Promoting Value Based Priorities
4497	Your VIP Registration Is Confirmed
4498	Put Yourself First
4499	What Are Their Emotional Hot Words Or Buttons
4500	Position Them As Your Students

Lynn and I hope that this "Think Tank" volume series of 500 Hot Phrases will helped you clearly paint your dreams, sell your ideas, and market your messages, propelling each of your ideas and projects toward incredible success. Watch for our next Volume!

We truly wish you the very best and look forward to hearing your success stories.

Concluding Thoughts:

Ever success is built upon a preparing a strong foundation, having a clear vision, and taking positive action each and every day. If you've been searching for a new lifestyle, then you'll find this book directive and inspirational. You can open it to any page and let that page help you rethink possibilities, consider new ideas, open new opportunities, and ultimately experience a more successful and fulfilling lifestyle.

Every problem has a solution! Regardless of your current situation or circumstance, know that you have the power and responsibility to redirect your life in any direction you choose. Simply start thinking about and research the kind of lifestyle that truly appeals to your heart. Begin your new journey by learning everything you can about your chosen subject. When you make that commitment, you'll open more unexpected doors to unique opportunities than imagined.

"Creative Thought Is The Only Reality
Everything Else Is Merely The By-Product Of That Thought."
- Walter Russell

So why not start thinking **BIGGER? It won't cost you any more.** It all starts by never allowing your current life's situation, environment, or so-called friends to limit your path to a happier, healthier, and successful life. After all, whose life is this?

Make a decision to focus on learning something new each and every day. Begin attracting your ideal lifestyle by doing something you love and enjoy. As difficult as it may be, don't allow money to limit your dreams. Focus on the kind of thoughts that make you feel good. Once you learn how to control your focus, you'll have a great chance to see your dreams take shape. You've finally learn to harness the power you always had within, a Universal Energy stream that flows 365/24/7 in any direction your project your thoughts, Good or Bad. Want proof? The thoughts you currently believe and project reflect the life you're currently living. Therefore, if your life isn't happening, change your thoughts, and change your life. It's something only you can hold, visualize, and project, living your dream come true.

Find yourself a mentor and spend more time with people who truly appreciate, support, and foster your dreams. Life may be short, but the thoughts we hold can make our life wider and more fulfilling.

20

About The Authors:

Richard and Lynn develop creative strategies that paint dreams, sell ideas, & market messages   Together, they present a unique team-approach, working side-by-side, helping clients pursue their passions while sharing their skills and diverse expertise as authors, artists, inventors, entrepreneurs, & Internet marketing education specialists.

Teaching by example, they mentor proven self-publishing services, graphic design, video production, domain acquisition, and marketing research of behalf of their company, RIVO Inc – RIVO Marketing, since 1997. They've created & produced hundreds of videos, self-published dozens of books on a wide variety of topics and created thousands of original works of fine art, while refining their Internet Marketing techniques, mentoring programs, and related business website development.

Their mission is to continually uncover new products and services, test new strategies, and network useful solutions with off and online entrepreneurs, small business owners, writers, local artists, models, teachers, students, and marketing professionals.

Their goal is to help clients create an action plan that discovers and connects the missing pieces of the success puzzle. The goals they foster create multiple streams of income for today's volatile economic climate. Their motto is: "Do the work once and allow the work to create additional streams of income for a lifetime."

Feel free to contact them if you have questions or would like to tap into their talents and expertise. They appreciate your feedback and look forward to hearing your success stories.

Contact:
Richard & Lynn Voigt - RIVO
I. M. Education Specialists

RIVO INC - RIVO Marketing
13720 West Keefe Avenue
Brookfield, Wisconsin 53005 – USA
Email: support@RIVOinc.com
Website: www.RIVObooks.com
Website: www.WisconsinGarden.com

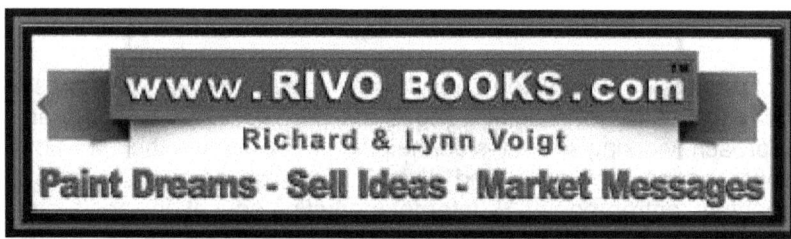

Visit Lynn's Garden: www.WisconsinGarden.com
view hundreds of great garden video blogs Tips

See Richard's Unique Artwork: www.RIVOart.com
view over 3,000 original Fine-Art compositions

Our Book Titles Now Available On Amazon:

THE GOLDEN VAULT OF MOTIVATIONAL QUOTATIONS
Words of Wisdom from The Greatest Minds & Leaders

BABY NAME .ME - 21,400 Names & Nicknames
For Family, Friends, Pets, Natural & Man-Objects

DOODLE DESIGNS Volumes 1-3
For Professionals & Kids Of All Ages
DOODLE DESIGNS – Vol. 1
DOODLE DESIGNS – Vol. 2
DOODLE DESIGNS Coloring Book Vol. 3

Work MORE Accomplish LESS Get FIRED!

ACTION HEADLINES That Drive Emotions – Volumes 1- 6
Paint Dreams, Sell Ideas & Market Your Message
Action Headlines That Drive Emotions Vol. 1
Action Headlines That Drive Emotions Vol. 2
Action Headlines That Drive Emotions Vol. 3
Action Headlines That Drive Emotions Vol. 4
Action Headlines That Drive Emotions Vol. 5
Action Headlines That Drive Emotions Vol. 6

IDIOMS – IDIOMS - IDIOMS
6,450 Popular Expressions That Put Words In Your Mouth

The CLICHÉ BIBLE - 8,400 Clichés For Sports Fanatics
& Lovers Of Popular Expressions

MORE THAN WORDS
5000+ Marketing Phrases That Sell

HYPNOTIC PHRASING
WARNING-This Book Teaches You How To Grab Eyeballs

YOUR RIGHT TO WEALTH
Becoming Wealthy Isn't Hard When You Know How

WI GARDEN – Let's Get Dirty
Our Wisconsin Garden Guide Promoting Delicious, Healthier Home-Grown Fresh Food, With Tools, Tips, & Ideas That Inspire Gardeners!

MONETIZE YOUR SOCIAL LIFE
Earn Extra Income While Having Fun Online

BABY NAMES
21,400 Unique Baby Names & Nicknames

FUNNY HEADLINES vol. 1
3,500 Outrageous Silly Brain Toots

FUNNY HEADLINES vol. 2
3,500 Outrageous Silly Brain Toots

JOBS
10,240 Career Paths That Can Change Your Life!

MONEY WORDS
Powerful Phrases That Million Dollar Copywriters Use To Make Piles Of Cash On Demand!

GARDEN QUOTATIONS
400 Garden Quotes From The Earth To Your Soul

HEADLINE STARTERS
175,000 Words That Paint Dreams, Sell Ideas, And Market Your Message

BABY NAMES
25,350 Baby Names & Nicknames For Your Family Friends & Pets
   697 pages 7,000 Names with Origin & Meaning plus Top 100 Names, And 2,000 Most Popular Names

CURIOUS WORDS
15,800 Words That Expand Your Mind And Change Your Life

INSPIRING THOUGHTS
That Inspire Happiness, Success & A Clearer Understanding Of Life

MARKETING EYEBALLS
100 Ideas That Can Add Unlimited Subscribers To Your Lists

SECOND OF FIVE
My Early Years- From Birth To High School

POWER PHRASES – Individual Volumes 1 - 10
500 Power Phrases That Trigger Greater Profits

POWER PHRASES Pro Edition – (Complete Series Volumes 1-10)
5000 Power Phrases That Trigger Greater Profits

CLAIM 500 MORE POWER PHRASES!

Thank you for purchasing this eBook and in doing so we would like to send you **500 More Red Hot Power Phrases for FREE!**

When you post a **positive review of this Book on Amazon Books** under this title you'll receive an additional **500 POWER PHRASES.** Your review may also be sent directly to us.

Your request must be received within 30-days of purchase. Once your positive Book review is posted and verified, simply email the following to (**500@RIVOinc.com**):

1. Full Name of Purchaser
2. Email address
3. Paypal Invoice Number
4. Copy of your posted Book Review*

Once we receive the above, we'll send you 500 Power Phrases **(PDF)** emailed to the address you provided.

Visit: www.RIVObooks.com for additional volumes as they become available including the Pro Edition of 5000 Red Hot Power Phrases that say what you mean to say and trigger greater profits.

Lynn and I look forward to your written comments and suggestions as we love hearing from each of our readers.

Richard & Lynn Voigt
RIVO Inc – RIVO Marketing
13720 West Keefe Avenue
Brookfield, Wisconsin 53005 USA
Telephone: (262) 783-5335
www.RIVObooks.com

P. S. If you love gardening, catch us on www.WisconsinGarden.com

*****NOTE**: This offer is valid providing it does not violate the terms of service of the entity with whom you made this purchase. Duplicate or incomplete entries will also not be eligible and this offer is limited to one request per email address. All eligible review submissions become the property of RIVO Inc - RIVO Marketing – RIVO books and may be used as promotional testimonials ads on RIVO Inc websites. This offer may be withdrawn at any time without prior written notice.

www.ingramcontent.com/pod-product-compliance
Lightning Source LLC
Chambersburg PA
CBHW060709280326
41933CB00012B/2367